Animal **Faces**

In the Forest

Hannah Kate Sackett

Illustrated by Martin Camm

Children's Publishing

Columbus, Ohio

 **Children's Publishing**

This edition published in the United States in 2003 by
McGraw-Hill Children's Publishing,
A Division of The McGraw-Hill Companies
8787 Orion Place
Columbus, Ohio 43240-4027

www.MHkids.com

Library of Congress Cataloging-in-Publication Data is on file with the publisher.

Created and produced by Firecrest Books Ltd.
in association with Martin Camm.

Art and Editorial Direction by Peter Sackett
Edited by Norman Barrett
Edited in the U.S. by Joanna Schmalz
U.S. Production by Nathan Hemmelgarn
Designed by Phil Jacobs
Color Separation by SC International Pte Ltd, Singapore

Printed and bound in Dubai.

ISBN 1-57768-428-1

1 2 3 4 5 6 7 8 9 10 FBL 06 05 04 03

Contents

Stag Beetle

The stag beetle lives among the fallen leaves and twigs, at the lowest level of the forest. The two-inch-long beetle takes its name from the male's long jaws, which look similar to a deer's antlers. These jaws sometimes grow to be almost as long as the beetle's body. The male beetles use these jaws to fight one another. The female beetles have much shorter jaws, but they are far stronger than the male's.

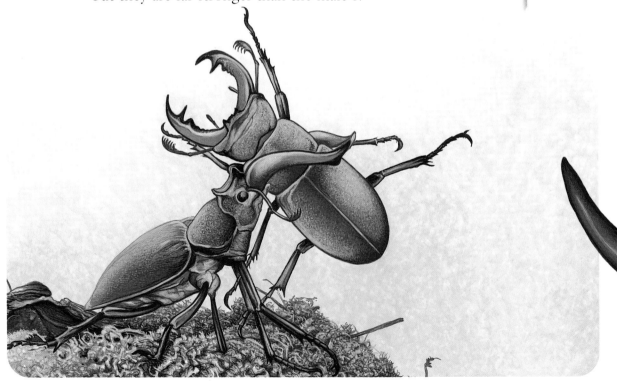

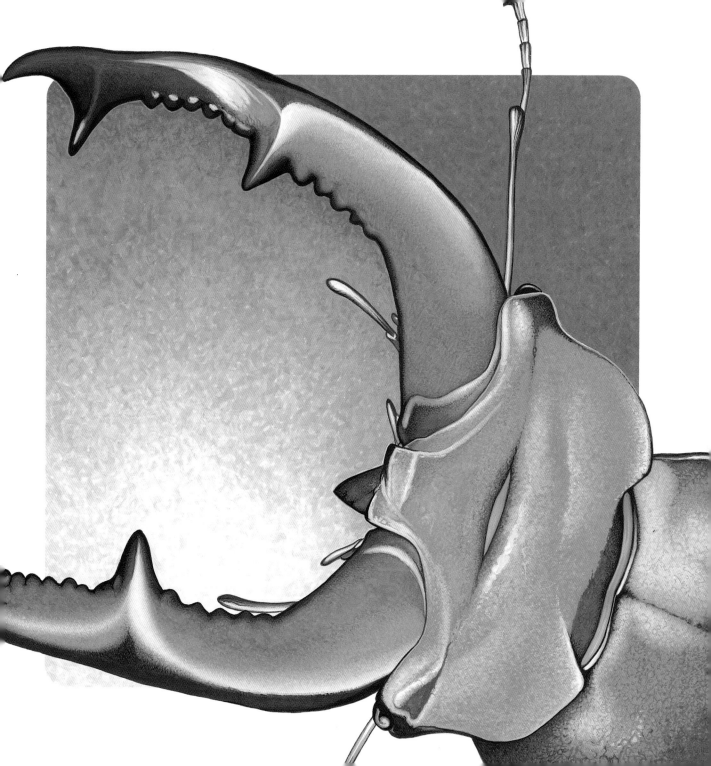

Wild Boar

Wild boar use their long, flat-ended snouts to find and dig up roots, bulbs, and insects lying just beneath the surface of the forest floor. Male boars defend themselves using two powerful, pointed teeth, called tusks. Females and their young do not have large tusks. They protect themselves by living in groups of about twenty boars. The faces and bodies of the young animals are marked with stripes. These markings allow them to blend with the shadows and hide from predators.

Badger

The badger uses its pointed snout to search among the leaves on the forest floor for food. It uses its teeth to eat worms and roots. If threatened, the badger bites its enemies. Male badgers often attack badgers who are not members of their own group, sometimes called a clan, by biting them. The Eurasian badgers, pictured here, have strong black and white stripes that mark their faces and help them blend into their surroundings.

Raccoon

The raccoon has a pointed nose, short, rounded ears, and mask-like black bands around its eyes. Until they are about 10 days old, newborn raccoons have no mask because they have little or no hair on their faces. Mother raccoons use their mouths to carry their young from place to place. They grasp the loose fur on the backs of the newborns' necks. Raccoons also use this gentle grip to steal birds' eggs, a food they commonly eat.

Lynx

The lynx stalks silently through the forest. This wild cat tracks its prey or lies hidden in wait in the undergrowth. When its prey is close, the lynx springs, closing its strong jaws and sharp teeth around the animal's neck. The lynx relies on its sharp senses of vision and hearing to find its prey. The lynx has long tufts of hair on its ears and cheeks. This fur serves as a sense organ, enhancing the lynx's hearing.

Black Bear

The black bear spends much of its time looking for food in the forest. It feeds on small animals, though its long tongue also enables it to eat nuts, fruit, honey, and ants. When looking for food, the bear relies on its strong senses of smell and hearing, rather than its small, weak eyes. Black bears can often be seen standing on their back legs, noses in the air, searching for the scent of food.

Wolf

The wolf's eyes have a special feature that reflect light somewhat like a mirror reflects an image. This helps the wolf see at night. Great hearing and a strong sense of smell make the wolf an effective hunter. In fact, the wolf is able to smell food more than a mile away. A wolf's most dangerous feature is its four sharp teeth, known as fangs. They are used for catching, wounding, and killing prey. Every one of a wolf's five senses is extremely sharp.

Beaver

Woodland streams, rivers, and lakes are home to the beaver, a creature known for its powerful teeth. The four large teeth at the front of a beaver's mouth have a very hard outer layer. Beavers use them to gnaw wood. That is because their diet is made up of leaves, bark, twigs, and roots. The beaver also uses wood to build its home, called a lodge. Beavers spend a lot of time in the water. To see underwater, the beaver has an extra, clear eyelid covering each eye. The beaver's rounded ears and small nostrils can close tightly to keep water out.

Moose

During the summer months, moose can often be seen in watery regions of the forest with their heads beneath the surface of a pond or stream, looking for water plants to eat. Moose have large noses, or muzzles, and flaps of skin, known as bells, which hang from their throats. The function of the bell is not known, though some scientists believe it is used to store fat. The male moose also has huge, flat antlers. Each autumn, males clash antlers in fights over who will mate with the females.

Wood Ant

Unlike many animals, the wood ant has jaws that move from side to side instead of up and down. These jaws are called mandibles. The ant uses them to catch and carry food. Mandibles are also useful for cutting through leaves and bark. Wood ants carry large numbers of leaves across the forest floor to build the mound, or nest, they live in. The most important feature of the ant's face are two stalks in front of its head called antennae. An ant uses its antennae as a sense organ—to smell, hear, taste, and touch.

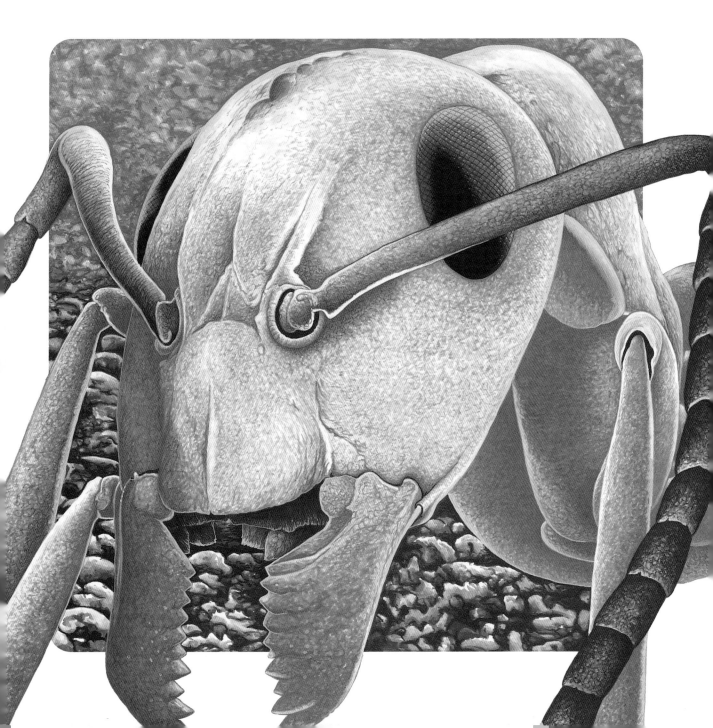

Tree Frog

The tree frog rarely climbs down to the forest floor. It stays among the leaves of the trees and waits for flying insects, catching them with its long, sticky tongue. The tree frog has dark stripes that start at each nostril and run along the sides of its body. These stripes help the tree frog to blend in to its surroundings. The female has a smooth, white throat, while the male's throat is darker in color. The tree frog's large eyes face forward. This helps the frog judge distances when jumping or climbing from tree to tree, or catching insects with its tongue.

Woodpecker

The upper part of the forest is home to a wide variety of birds. Among them is the woodpecker. This bird has a long, sharp, and very hard bill. It is used to drill into the wood and bark of trees to build a nest or find food. The woodpecker also uses its bill to drum on hollow logs or branches. Scientists think that this is their way of sending signals to other birds. Special muscles on the bird's face absorb most of the shock of their pecking. These muscles prevent the woodpecker from damaging its skull.

Crossbill

The crossbill makes its nest high in the treetops. This small bird takes its name from the way in which the tips of its bill cross. This unusual bill allows the crossbill to get its favorite food, pine seeds. These seeds are tucked inside pine cones. The crossbill's strong and specially designed bills can retrieve them. Large flocks of crossbills often descend on a single tree to snap up the ripe seeds.

Facts Behind the Faces

The animals in this book live in forests in the northern parts of the world. Their faces and their senses are uniquely designed to allow them to survive in the forest. This part of the book tells you about these animals—where they live, their relatives, their eating habits, and their enemies. From the stag beetle living on the forest floor to the crossbill flying through the treetops, here are the facts behind the faces.

Stag Beetle
Family: There are about 1,250 kinds of stag beetles.
Where they live: The giant stag beetle is native to the United States.
Size: The stag beetle is about 2 inches in length.
Special feature: The females lay their eggs in dead wood, which is eaten by the beetle larvae when they hatch.

Wild Boar
Family: The wild boar is a member of the pig family.
Where they live: Wild boar are native to Europe, Asia, and northern Africa.
What they eat: Roots, fruit, acorns, eggs, mice, worms, and beetles.
Size: 5.25-6 feet in length; males weigh up to 450 pounds.
Enemies: They are hunted for sport and farmed for their meat.

Badger
Family: The weasel family includes badgers, otters, skunks, and minks.
Types of badger: American badger, Eurasian badger, and hog badger.
Where they live: In northern Asia, Europe, and North America.
What they eat: Earthworms, bulbs, nuts, fruit, and small animals.
Size: Their bodies can grow to about 32 inches in length.

Raccoon
Family: The raccoon family includes raccoons, ringtails, and coatis.
Where they live: North America and South America.
What they eat: Fruit, nuts, eggs, crayfish, insects, and small animals.
Size: 24-42 inches in length.
Enemies: Human beings hunt raccoons for sport and for their fur.

Lynx
Family: The lynx is a member of the cat family.
Types of lynx: The Canadian, Eurasian, and Iberian lynx.
Where they live: The lynx is found in Asia, Europe, and North America.
What they eat: Reindeer, elk, hares, birds, sheep, and fish.
Size: Up to 4.25 feet in length, with a tail 1.5-3 inches long.

Black Bear
Family: The black bear is a member of the bear family.
Other bears: Brown bears, Asian black bears, and polar bears.
What they eat: Acorns, fruit, nuts, honey, fish, and small mammals.
Size: 5-6 feet in length.
Special features: Some black bears have brown, gray, or even white fur.

Wolf
Family: The wolf is a member of the dog family.
Types of wolf: Gray wolves, including timber and tundra wolf; red wolf.
Where they live: Remote areas of North America, Europe, and Asia.
What they eat: Caribou, deer, and moose.
Special features: Wolves live and hunt together in groups called packs.

Beaver
Family: Beavers are one of the largest members of the rodent family.
Other rodents: Mice, rats, squirrels, prairie dogs, and porcupines.
Where they live: North America, Asia, and Europe.
Size: 3-4 feet long, and 40-95 pounds in weight.
Special features: Their front teeth never stop growing.

Moose

Family: The moose is the largest member of the deer family.
Other deer: Red deer, reindeer, and white-tailed deer.
Where they live: North America, northern Europe, and Asia.
What they eat: Plants growing in woodlands and in water.
Size: Up to 7.5 feet tall, and weighing as much as 1,800 pounds.

Wood Ant

Family: There are around 15,000 different kinds of ants in the ant family.
Where they live: Worldwide, except for very cold regions.
What they eat: Plants and other insects.
Special features: Two long stalks at the front of an ant's head, called antennae, are used for smelling, hearing, tasting, and touching.

Tree Frog

Family: This species is one of around 600 kinds of tree frogs.
Where they live: North America, South America, and Europe.
What they eat: Flying insects.
Size: Up to 2 inches.
Special features: Changes color to blend with its background.

Woodpecker

Family: The woodpecker family has 200 kinds of woodpeckers.
Other woodpeckers: Ivory-billed, greater spotted, and golden-tailed.
Where they live: Worldwide, except Australia and Madagascar.
What they eat: Insects, fruit, nuts, and acorns.
Special features: Long, sticky tongue helps extract larvae from trees.

Crossbill

Family: The crossbill is a member of the finch family.
Other crossbills: Red, or American, crossbill and white-winged crossbill.
Where they live: Asia, Europe, and North America.
What they eat: Pine seeds, plant shoots and buds, and insects.
Size: Around 6 inches in length.

Index